ICKY BUG
SHAPES

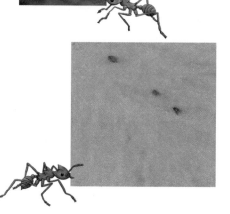

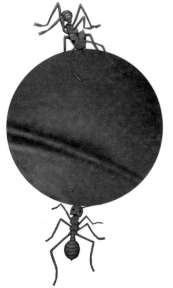

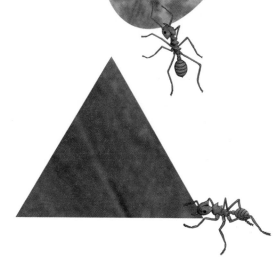

by Jerry Pallotta
Illustrated by Shennen Bersani

SCHOLASTIC INC.

New York   Toronto   London   Auckland   Sydney   Mexico City   New Delhi   Hong Kong   Buenos Aires

Thank you to Barbara J. Pye
—Jerry Pallotta

For my family, Kerrin, Bethany, Karlene, Ryan, and Tom
—Shennen Bersani

Library of Congress Cataloging-in-Publication Data available.

ISBN 0-439-38918-6

12 11 10 9 8   7   8/0

Printed in the U.S.A.   40
First printing, March 2003

Leafcutter ants live underground.
They live in huge nests.
Some of these nests hold more than one million ants.
These ants are on their way to work.

Every ant has a job to do. Some leafcutter ants are scouts.
They tell the other leafcutter ants where to find the nice leaves.
The leafcutter ants start walking up the tree.

Up they go toward the juicy leaves.
The ants with big jaws do the cutting.
The largest ants are the guards. They protect the other ants.
All leafcutter ants work as a team.

TRIANGLE

Leafcutter ants have jaws like scissors.
This ant just cut out a triangle.
A triangle is a shape with three straight sides.
Each side of this triangle is the same length.

Here is a triangle spider. Most spiders are round.
As you can see, this spider has a body shaped like a triangle.
The triangle spider uses its thorny front legs to catch bugs.

No!
This is not an alien from another planet!
It is the face of a praying mantis.
This insect's head is shaped
like a triangle.

Now that you are experts at finding triangles, look at this bug. Can you see a triangle shape somewhere on its body?

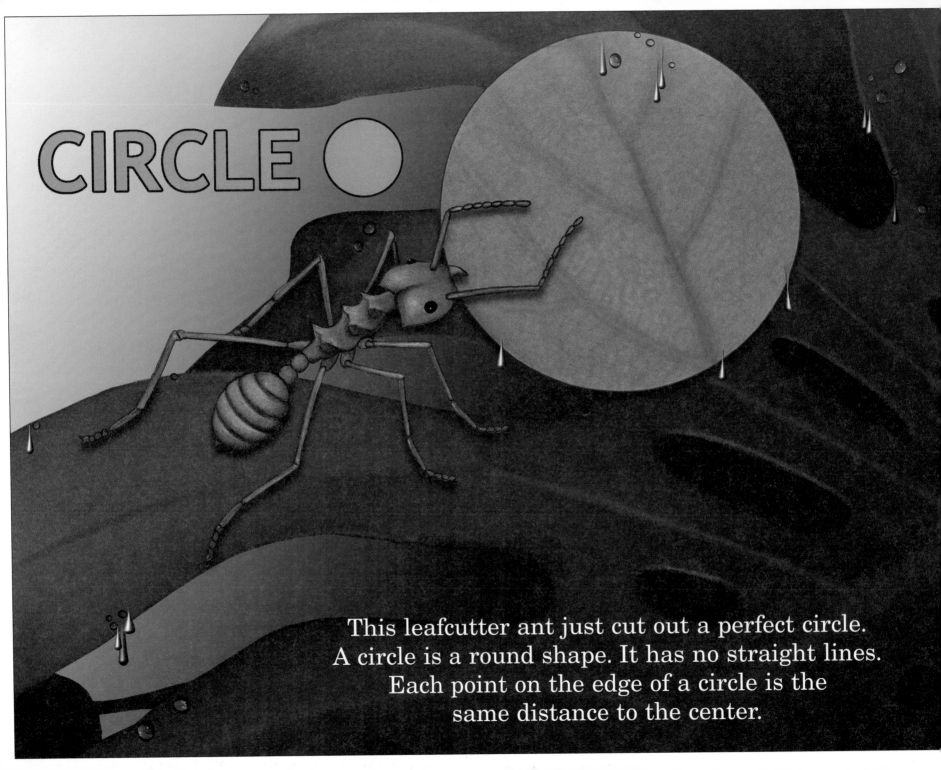

CIRCLE

This leafcutter ant just cut out a perfect circle.
A circle is a round shape. It has no straight lines.
Each point on the edge of a circle is the
same distance to the center.

These colorful butterflies have circular shapes on the underside of their wings. Why would they have them? Are they a warning to stay away? Are they fake eyes? Do the circles attract other butterflies? No one is really sure.

Bumblebees are fuzzy all over. These are not bumblebees.
They are carpenter bees. They have a smooth shiny abdomen.
Carpenter bees make their nests by chewing holes into wood.
They can even chew a circle into the side of a house.

Here is a weevil from southeast Asia.
It looks like someone designed it in art class.
There are shapes everywhere in nature.

SQUARE

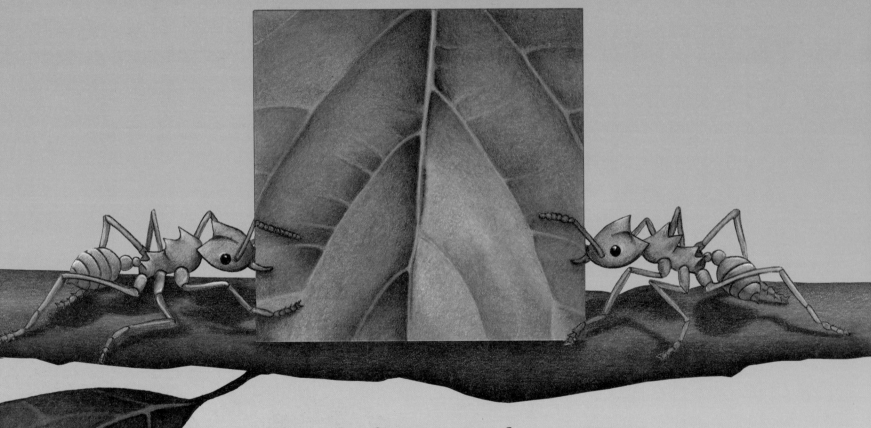

These leafcutter ants have cut out a square.
A square is a shape with four sides that are the same length.
All four corners of a square are at right angles,
just like the pages of this book.

Here are two moths back-to-back.
Their bodies are positioned just
right to make a square. A square is a very hard
shape to find in the wild.

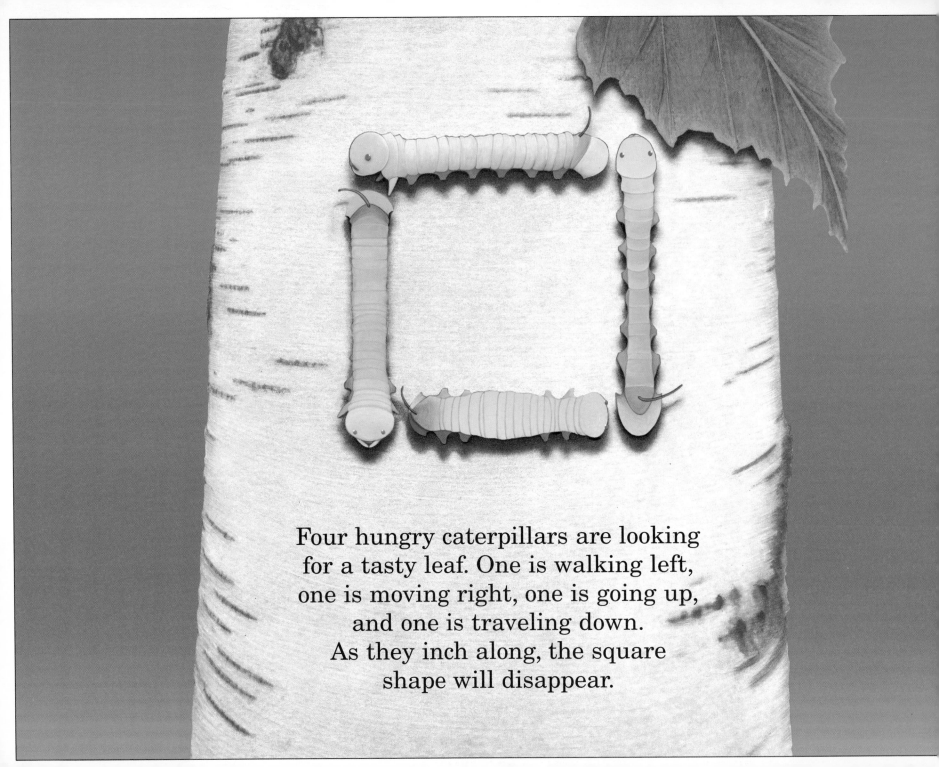

Four hungry caterpillars are looking
for a tasty leaf. One is walking left,
one is moving right, one is going up,
and one is traveling down.
As they inch along, the square
shape will disappear.

Here are two lacewings.
They have stopped to take a rest on a clothesline.
Each lacewing has four wings. Their long, skinny
hind wings line up to form a square.

OVAL

This leafcutter ant cut out an oval.
An oval is a shape that looks like a stretched circle.
The wind just blew this ant off the tree.
Whoa! There it goes!

Take a look at this grasshopper.
Can you find an oval shape on its body?
You're right! Its eye is shaped like an oval.

Here are some oval-shaped ladybugs.
Most ladybugs have polka dots. These Australian
ladybugs have zigzag designs on their backs.

Longhorn beetles have unusually long antennae.
These are so long they stretch around the beetle's
body and make an oval shape.

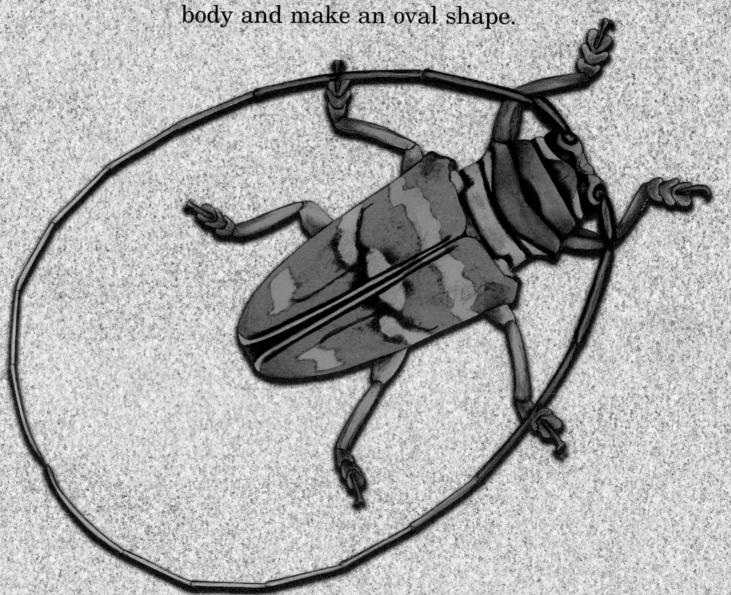

RECTANGLE

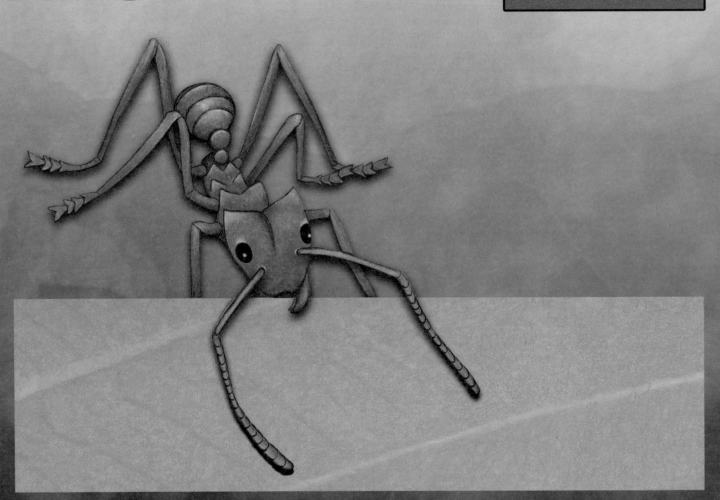

Here is a rectangle. A rectangle has four sides and four right angles. The sides next to each other are different lengths. The opposite sides are the same length.

Walking sticks do not look like bugs.
They look like twigs or sticks.
Two of them are walking from one branch to another.
They form a rectangle.

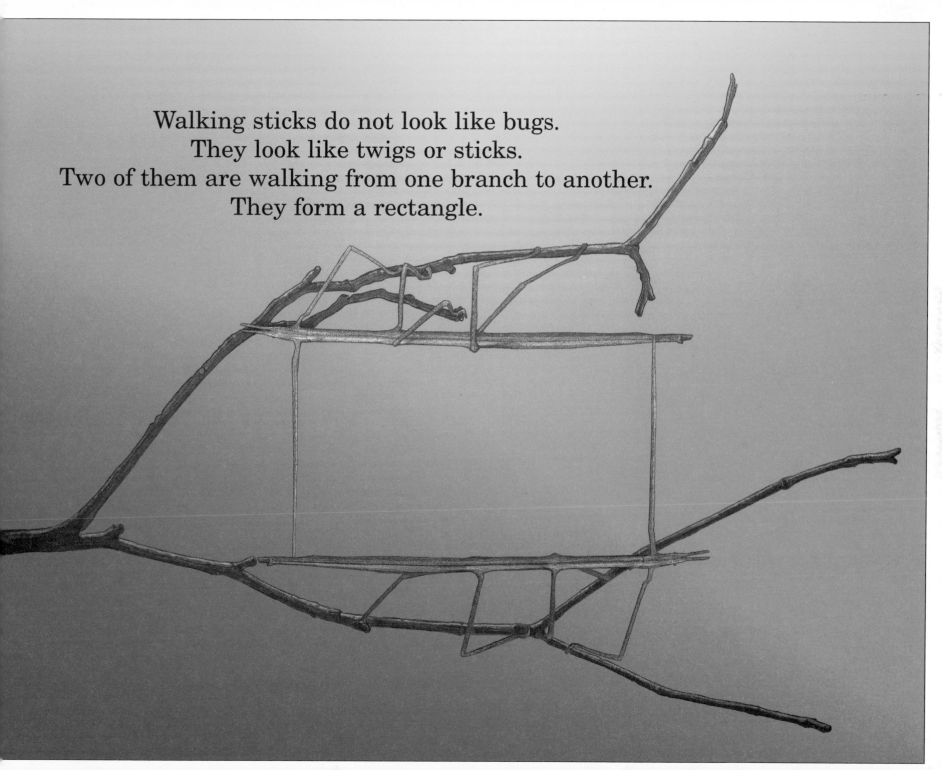

The net-casting spider is very clever. It builds a web and then throws it on the bug it's trying to catch. Sometimes the web is shaped like a rectangle.

This cicada has rectangle designs on its wings.
Cicadas are the loudest of all insects.
They make a buzzing sound.

PENTAGON

There are leafcutter bees, too!
These leafcutter bees cut out a pentagon shape.
A pentagon is a shape that has five sides.

A mother beetle just laid her eggs in the shape of a pentagon.
The markings on the eggs make them look like happy faces.
More bugs coming soon!

HEXAGON

Sometimes leafcutter ants cut flower petals, too. This leafcutter ant is carrying a hexagon. Hexagons have six sides.

Hexagons are very common in nature.
Bees and wasps make hexagon-shaped nests.
These wasps chewed wood to make this paper nest.

After a long walk, the leafcutter
ants are coming home. They are carrying all
these shapes down to their nest.

You should recognize the shapes the ants on this page are carrying.
The rectangle, the oval, the square, the circle,
and the triangle will soon be underground.

Inside the nest, the smaller leafcutter ants chop the leaves into tiny pieces. The pile of chewed leaves decays, and fungus grows. The leafcutter ants eat the fungus. Oooh, delicious! They grow their own food. Wow! Leafcutter ants are farmers!